To Stacey
& Kristian

May these few
thoughts
resinate
with you

Respectfully

[signature]

July 2016

Meditation

the art & act of mindfulness

with
Henry Landry, Author, Buddhist Teacher, Messenger

authorHOUSE®

AuthorHouse™
1663 Liberty Drive
Bloomington, IN 47403
www.authorhouse.com
Phone: 1 (800) 839-8640

Published by AuthorHouse 03/15/2016

ISBN: 978-1-5049-8259-7 (sc)
ISBN: 978-1-5049-8258-0 (e)

Library of Congress Control Number: 2016904119

Print information available on the last page.

"Meditation natures pharmacy."
"On the pathway spiritual sustain-ability & peaceful means."

1. Meditation--Buddhism. I. Title.
2. Self Growth
3. Spiritual Awareness

Website: www.VIRetreats.com
Twitter: Buddha_Now FaceBook: Nichiren
Buddha Society FaceBook: Henry Landry
Podcast: Meditation Now
Donations: www.begiving.ca/charities/nichirenbuddha

Sharing Sessions

MAKE THIS BOOK YOUR FRIEND

Meditation is the Art and Act that brings knowledge and better health realizations. Meditation is an art of discipline, hope and joy. In the beginning it takes patience and an understanding that "I may or may not get the results I have read or heard about elsewhere." The master key, is that in "calming, cultivating and controlling the mind" we will find peace of mind, which we shall know as a treasure. prosperity.

Meditation is an offering made up in modules of practical knowledge when taken together with practice, will take us to places we have only dreamed of; it will bring our visions into new holistic perspective, from time to time, it will bring a quietude of healthful giving and joyous feelings beyond words into the world of bliss.

The Meditation Exercises throughout this book hopefully bring us beyond the beginning of mindful awareness allowing us to go deeper into our meditation zone. The exercises offer the practitioner an opportunity to listen and focus on *"one point"*. Realizing meditation is an offering that has an active practical application in order to complete itself; it is not about doing nothing. These exercises give us the ability to take up *InSights* that lead to greater understanding of our daily life and the world around us. A goal of meditation is strength of self, with the empowerment of constant awareness and mindful BE-ing.

When we contemplate and meditate a little each day we open up our *miracle mind* to all that is. In meditating we walk the pathway to conquer all life's challenges. One meditation at a time, we build a life of indestructible happiness.

Meditation takes us to that place of no doubt, no fear, no worry! Meditation is about this life and the life beyond; enjoy, celebrate know that you are interdependent with the eternal!

In the beginning Meditation takes effort, the rewards are worthwhile!

"When we meditate, we join temporary human mind, with universal eternal Mind, this is why we call it the act and art of mindfulness"

Introduction

A purpose of meditation is the practice of watching and capturing new ideas, feelings, thoughts that arise from concentration and using them in our daily life. Meditation is about cultivating and controlling our miracle mind, it is about the energy of breath! It is an offering that brings much benefit as it gathers merit towards this life and the ones after.

Meditation is an Art, and artful imaging takes work. The good news is our Meditation becomes habit and like most habits the mind soon enough remembers to enter the meditation zone quite easily. The details of "letting go" become easier.

For beginners, one purpose of meditation is to calm the busy mind through mindful cultivation and control through mindful practices. Biologically the brain that contains One's mind is an electro-magnetic dynamo with a multitude of electro synapses firing on and off constantly; understanding this physical aspect of the brain/mind helps us understand and respect our busy mind.

Meditation, like any new habit, takes patience, time, perseverance and right mindfulness to succeed. For most new comers the ideas behind the practice are not easy. However, the benefits are multi-fold: better breathing, stronger heart, healthful balance all round, spiritual awakening. One of the first virtues one acquires with the practice of meditation is humility, for cultivating and controlling the mind is not for the light hearted. To realize *the Act and*

Art of Meditation one follows the bodily hormonal energy flow and the spiritual vital life force within the bodily nervous system. This cultivation takes discipline, time and a little practice each and everyday. The rewards are multiple fascinating and beautiful!

The great news is we are each of us gardeners of our personal domain. This is where the various forms of Meditation come in to assist all who are willing to learn an empowering new habit form, one that is proven to reduce stress, give the heart a calmer beat, one that in time becomes much wanted just like that morning coffee or tea.

Enjoy this vast topic which is more than 6,000 years old, it truly has a purpose, a method and a practice that will make One's life easier, healthier and more rewarding.

Art of Meditation

Breath Always the Breath

Yogic Breath a Master Key To Meditation

The Hindrances

Body Position, Body Scan Exercise

Tai Chi - Power of Numbers - Meditation

Oneness Meditation

Way of Buddhist Meditation

It's About You

*"We want to free the body by energizing
and relaxing the body, so it will be
able to let go, so we can let go of our
attachments" HL*

THE ART OF MEDITATION

Think of contemplative meditation as layers of dirt, rock, bronze, silver and gold. To get at the gold there is much sifting to do. Think of all Meditation as an offering. Try to Realize, your mind is actually pure, but it is filled with the Five Entrances: eyes, nose, ears, tongue and skin. It is the Sixth consciousness called Volition that controls the entrances of sensation, and also allows us to go beyond emotion into the Seventh Level of Consciousness, the Lotus Land of bliss. The Meditation of a thousand ways!

BREATH ALWAYS THE BREATH

"Life is a series of breaths, if there is breath there is life, if there is no breath, there is no life" Anon

In our act of inhalation, when we breath properly, the muscles expand the lungs. Proper control of our respiratory muscles results in better health. Proper breathing means breathing through our nostrils, not through our mouth. Being fully aware of breathing, we breath in and pause or hold, breathing out, we pause between breaths, from deep breathing to mindful breathing.

In our early stages, because of our busy minds, we count our breaths when our mind wanders, we come back to counting our breaths. In the beginning we may need to do this over and over as we learn to cultivate and control our emotional minds. We go from beginners breath, counting breaths, watching breath, to a calmness of breath where we are not even aware we are breathing; able to come back to breath whenever the emotional mind wanders, interrupting our insight, and blocking the higher levels of deep meditation.

YOGIC MEDITATIVE BREATH

Do not let this exercise confuse you, few of us realize that in proper breathing there are four parts to every breath that lead us to no breath. We warm up with our secret meditative breath as we prepare to go to our meditation zone. As mentioned there are four parts of every breath we take. Inflowing - healthful energy gathering - pause - Outflowing and toxic energy releasing - pause; thousands of years old yoga practice for 'healing' of body and mind. The suggested inhale is to the count of six or eight. We hold the intake breath so it can energize the lungs. We hold for a half count. We exhale our carbon dioxide and toxins for full count and pause before taking in the new oxygen.

We inhale for Full count, Hold for Half count, Exhale for Full count, Hold for Half count. When we practice this for four or five minutes then the body and mind hindrances will, for the most part, work themselves out because we are paying attention to the counting of the breath. At first the counting of breaths may seem strange but it is one manner of cultivating and controlling the mind. Whenever we find a busy mind, we come back to counting the breath. Do not be confused by the counting. If you find this difficult simply say I AM breathing

3

in, holding the breath, I AM breathing out, holding the breath, I AM meditating for health, happiness and prosperity whatever our focus for the present meditation.

We set up our mindful life energy breathing with this simple 6-3-6-3, Counting in Six, holding Three, Six out, holding three, Six In, holding three, Six Out, Three Hold, doing this with repetition to control the busy mind. With practice we may be able to increase this to a natural 8-4-8-4, or even 10–5-10-5, depending on our metabolism. The secret wisdom here is in the *"Energy Flow, or vital life force."* The breathing In and Out only provides partial Health care for the body, it is the holding period between breathe that increases the flow of healthful energy to all parts of the body. This early stage of breath control is not meditation, it is setting up the body and mind to go into meditation.

When you see someone in very good health into their eighties and nineties one of the main reasons for their balance is correct deep breathing. Remember, once we go into our meditation zone, we will hardly know we are breathing, until the mind wanders and we need to come back to the breath.

THE HINDRANCES

In the beginning, as we sit to meditate the mind wants to wander, the body wants to twitch, this is normal the body wants in on the action even when you are sleeping which is why we turn over in our sleep and within our dream states. These meditative hindrances are actually quite easy to control, in a short time, with practice. The important point about the hindrances in the beginning is to just let them be. Acknowledge them and go on with meditating.

Next, understand that our meditation will depend on how quiet our mind is. In the beginning this will be challenging, more so for some than others. If we have had a stressful day, we may expect our settling time to take longer as we have not enough practice to go directly into the Meditation Zone. BE Free, simply be in the Moment. Realize this Gift of Time, our Meditation Time, this time for us. This Gift belongs to us! Put away all doubt, put away fear and know this is the right medicine for Mind, Body and Spirit.

Within the body is not One Mind, but Two Minds, not Two Minds, but One Mind. This is to say, you have the Mind of Thought in the upper brain and the Mind of Energy located about three fingers just below your frontal rib cage, this is called the Solar Plexus. In meditation the idea is to get these two minds to work as One. We can start by holding a *Visualization Point.* [This is for sitting meditation, not walking meditation.] We will be discussing Visualization techniques in greater detail later. For now the "visualization point" is up to you, a candle flame [the centre dark blue], a crystal glass with clean water, the beauty within a favourite picture, a flower, a piece of fruit, the glow of incense.

In time and with practice we are able to pick a visualization point through our awareness. Just BE! Breathing gently Now, in/out, in/out, in/out, body relaxed, we meditate towards our Visualization Point and begin to Meditate without moving the mind, concentrating on One visual point! Don't be disappointed how quickly we realize we are unable to do this for even a full minute without mind wandering, we are after all only beginning, this is the introduction of Ways and Means.

Body Position

Our eyes relaxed and softly open, half closed or closed lightly towards the tip of our nose. Our hands joined, toes and hands touching lightly, the energy body of circulation joined. We are comfortable, meditation should be a quiet relaxation. Sitting in a position of comfort, on a meditation bench or cushion, on a chair, on the floor, this is our meditation, let's be comfortable. Before beginning meditation it is always wise to stretch the body a little, roll the neck in a complete circle, move it left to right, right to left, up and down, stretch the feet, roll and stretch the wrists and fingers, now take a take a few deep breaths, always through the nostrils. This sends the right message to the body, it awakens it to the fact that a new action is about the take place.

Body Scan - An Exercise

We begin to relax the body by sending our intake of new oxygen to the various parts of the body. Sending the intake of new oxygen, our new breaths to our feet, ankles, lower and upper legs, our solar plexus [three fingers below our frontal rib cage,] the lungs, the breast, the shoulders, the upper arms, the lower arms, the hands, the fingers, the bottom of the back, working our way up to the shoulders, relaxing the face, the eyes, the forehead, the neck [very important] now moving into the brain, relaxing the mind. Relaxing the muscles, quiet letting go of all tension. [For beginners this process will take 15 or 20 minutes, with practice this whole process will take 3 to 4 minutes for both body and mind]

Our hands may be positioned to be clasped together and touching our breast, or with hands folded one over the other resting in our lap, just below our solar plexus, thumbs touching.

Eyes can be lightly closed or golden eye, that is slightly open to concentrate on an object such as the light of a candle, a piece of fruit, a flower, the glow of incense as you reflect and send loving energy to the many parts of the body.

Sitting: Use a meditation bench, cushions that keep the spine straight, whatever will allow you to be comfortable for periods of time.
Hands: May be folded together [namaste position] on the chest, held lightly in bonding one hand on top of the other facing upward thumb to thumb or simply holding one hand on each leg relaxing.

Back: Our back must be straight and upright, no slouching.
Neck: Again, already having freed the neck of strain in our warm up exercise, we simply hold head up with ability to gaze at any object of our "visualization," mandala, candle light, flower.

Eyes: Gaze on candle, a piece of fruit, a visualizing light, a word stone; when they close softly open them back to the focal point for balance and visualization of objects in our meditation.

Mouth: Lightly closed for inward breath through nostrils, forming an "O" lightly open for exhale of breath, all in a natural motion.

Our Body position then, comfortable with spine, back, neck and head straight; alert, relaxed, always with the breath as our core.

BUDDHIST BREATH MEDITATION EXERCISE

Preparing to enter meditative mindfulness, sitting straight we focus our attention on making ten breaths as one thought, we rest in the quiet, then we focus our attention on making ten breaths our second thought like this, 1 inhale and hold - exhale and hold - 2 inhale and hold - exhale and hold - 3 - inhale and hold - exhale and hold - 4 - inhale and hold - exhale and hold - 5 - inhale and hold - exhale and hold - 6 - inhale and hold - exhale and hold - 7 - inhale and hold - exhale and hold - 8 - inhale and hold - exhale and hold - 9 - inhale and hold - exhale and hold - 10 - inhale and hold - exhale and hold - *pausing now - restful with no thoughts*, then 10 - inhale and hold - exhale and hold - 9 - inhale and hold - exhale and hold - 8 - inhale and hold - exhale and hold - 7 - inhale and hold - exhale and hold - 6 - inhale and hold - exhale and hold - 5 - inhale and hold - exhale and hold - 4 - inhale and hold - exhale and hold - 3 - inhale and hold - exhale and hold - 2 - inhale and hold - exhale and hold - 1 - inhale and hold - exhale and hold; now we enter quiet mindfulness and hold onto it as long as we can.... when the miracle mind comes back to disturb us we can once again go back to the counting until restful once again. *Tien Tai Chi'I 538 - 597 c.e.*

POWER OF NUMBERS ~ *TAI CHI* ~ MEDITATION EXERCISE

The Chinese have an ancient Chinese numeric code they use as vibrational self healing through sound meditation, much like we have done with our body scan. It goes like this: Sahn sahn jeo liu bah yow woo - Sahn sahn jeo liu bah yow woo [which translates as 3 9 6 8 1 5] it is repeated with each meditation like this: May the Buddhist energies join with my body - *Sahn sahn jeo liu bah yow woo - protect my chest and lungs - Sahn sahn jeo liu bah yow woo* - May the Buddhist energies protect my lower abdomen - *Sahn sahn jeo liu bah yow woo* - May the Buddhist energies protect my ribs and sides - Sahn sahn jeo liu bah yow woo - May the Buddhist energies protect my navel and solar plexus - *Sahn sahn jeo liu bah yow woo* - May the Buddhist energies protect my brain and head - Sahn sahn jeo liu bah yow woo - May the Buddhist energies protect my stomach, spleen and mid abdomen - *Sahn sahn jeo liu bah yow woo!*

MASTER KEYS TO MEDITATION

Two ways of handing meditation are Visualization Focus and Awareness Based Technique. BEing fully aware of our mindfulness, we go with our miracle mind and follow the pathways of awareness, but with non attachment. Seeking *one point of focus* for our meditation, as our mind wanders keep coming back to breath again, and again, training the mind until we are masters of our mind, we do not let our emotional mind control us, we become the master of our mind. Our one point of mindfulness can be very simple. Make this Love, Peace, Joy, Purity, Sun, Moon, Happiness, or any number of points. When we can let go, we will reach the mindfulness of no mind!

We keep coming back to our One Point, over and over as we work to achieve the Seventh level of consciousness, Bliss Energy. Relax as we constantly come back to our starting point, our breath. As we advance with discipline and practice all this changes into just BE-ing with all that is; letting go of everything that has been our tools in getting into the meditation zone. The two truths of conditional existence and eternal mindfulness merge. The mind being at peace and undisturbed by the hindrances. We are reminded this takes discipline, time and patience.

We can see now that our insight depends on discipline, the ability to harmonize mind energy with nervous energy which we will discuss at more length later. This is the Pathway to peaceful mind. Mind wandering at first is natural, let it happen, follow it for awhile, then we watch our breathing. Later, we will learn how to use a mantra, as our second "one point" of reference on the way to the MED Zone. It takes discipline, effort and work, just like any new habit; but have no doubt in time we become masters of our meditative mind.

The lamp of Buddhist philosophy is the concept of Oneness. The oneness of the person and the law, the oneness of life and it's environment, the oneness of body and mind, the oneness of birth and death. One cannot separate the individual from the community, the community from the country, there is One earth. One cannot separate the self from the environment. An awareness of this Oneness is obtained through meditation and in chanting a mantra like the Infinite Title of the *Lotus Sutra of Nam-Myoho-Renge-Kyo,* the Oneness of this moment of now, confirmation of the Buddha's highest teachings!

Ten Qualities of Meditation

1] daily practice 2] sincerity 3] self-respect 4] simplicity 5] discipline 6] correct place 7] non attachment {no doubt} 8] contentment 9] faith 10] patience.

Seven Classic Types of Meditation

1] breath 2] visualization 3] point [chakra] 4] sound [mantra] chanting 5] movement [mudra] e.g. Tai Chi 6] devotional 7] direct essence of contemplation [great silence].

Early Stages of Meditation - Development or *dhyana's,*

First Stage: A feeling of calmness, lightness, comfort, thoughts passing through, somewhat aware, peaceful

Second Stage: Non attachment, no specific thinking, lightness, acceptance, inner joy, great peace

Third Stage: Oneness with All, beyond the senses of touch, smell, hearing, seeing, feeling, Seventh Consciousness When one is fortunate to Realize Light Energy, it is a sign of One's virtue of purity - free from our human sensuality, awakening to emit light, peaceful, calm, achieving Bodhi nature.

> *"When the mind does not stop, it is like practising archery; gradually we learn to hit the target"*

Tien Ta'i Chi'I 538 - 597 c.e.

WAY OF BUDDHIST MEDITATION

Buddhist Meditation includes symbolic offerings including candles, incense, water and evergreens. The greens symbolize the truth of life's existence and our responsibility to work within the laws of nature and our environment. Candles stand for the truth and light of non- substantiality or the latent potential of life. Also, they represent the property of wisdom and the potential wisdom each of us has to seek our innate Buddha nature. Incense represents lighting the truth of the Middle Way, the property of the Universal Law. This is a fundamental truth to which the Buddha is enlightened, this is the balance of body, mind and spirit.

The Tenth Chapter in the *Lotus Sutra* [A Teacher of the Law] mentions the act of burning of incense before the Buddha. We place fresh water before our holy space each morning, stating: *"I offer this water and these offerings in devotion to the Buddha Dharma of Sowing and express my gratitude for all benefits, whether I see them or not."* The water is left throughout the day and removed just before evening meditation. Water has always been regarded as an important ingredient of our health and well being. Food, such as fruit is also an offering we make to show our thanksgiving, gratitude and appreciation for our health. Flowers and other offerings may also be made in a sincere manner of support and love.

The object of Ones meditation is to realize energy far beyond the miracle mind" HL

The important thing in practising meditation is not to worry about the mental state we are in, or the length of time we are going to practice, or whether we are doing it correctly or not; we *just do it*. We will achieve personal empowerment with practice!

It is important the we be washed and clean. Wearing light clothing, we gently excise the body, we settle ourselves, calmly breathing in and out with the rhythm of our heart-beat as we prepare to enjoy our empowerment and communication with the *universal mystic Law*.

All our meditation energy goes out into our universe being heard and responded too. Naturally, we want a clean place, a respectful place to practice. Also, we make sure others respect this energy [holy] space. It is suggested that we have no solid food for several hours before meditation.

Meditation has been in practice for many thousands of years and while I would never tell you how to realize your spiritual nature, this book does offer several of the Buddhist ways of meditative practice. We will learn for example about the Infinite Title of the Lotus Sutra and how chanting of this mantra: *Namu Myoho Renge Kyo*, can be part of a Walking Meditation, part of our meditative concentration that leads to contemplation and letting go into the harmony of universal mindfulness.

We know we have achieved an *enlightened* moment when we enter a blissful state of mind and body that carries the self through to a higher world of consciousness. This is most difficult to explain with words, it is a state of being that we *Realize*. Buddhist's call this the Eighth World of Realization.

We must treat our meditation with the same attitude as if our most cherished, loved, family member or friend were coming for a visit. Then even if we are in a bad state of mind, our energy flow will alter as we think of the goodness of friendship, love and true self.

"Becoming calm is called Stopping;
becoming Aware is called Seeing"
Tien Tai Chi'I

*"The ability to keep the mind on One Point
without wavering is called concentration"*
HL

*Daily Practice – 20 Minutes a Day,
out of 24 hours
So Simple, So Difficult!*

**CONTEMPLATION OF BODY,
MIND & SOUL**

Deep Meditative Joy

Introduction to Levels of Consciousness

The Hindrances – Part Two

Our Nervous Energy System

Science and the Universal Law

Going There

It's Still About You

"The object of our meditation practice: seeking the full health of body, mind and spirit, with practice awakening, arising to new strengths, wealth within, experience is our teacher " HL

Deep Meditative JOY   The Sounds Of Silence

We are all gardeners! Each responsible for the seeds within our garden, be that anger, happiness, suffering or joy. Like a garden we find ourselves either at the planting, the maturing or the harvest in the Seasons of our life and with our desire to understand our purpose. Regardless of your view of meditation, at this stage, it is important to understand that with practice you are awakening the power of compassion and *releasing the root of suffering.*

Introduction To Levels Of Consciousness

We all recognize the first Five levels of consciousness: hearing, seeing, touching, smelling and tasting. The Sixth Level is called Volition, which is the scientific reality of enabling us to use one or more of the first five levels of consciousness. The most beautiful 7th Level of Consciousness is what Yogins and Buddhists call the Bliss Level, here we are in touch with our inner soul, for a moment or more feeling weightless, filled with the Light of Eternity, sometimes receiving answers to doubts and life's challenges, sometimes just BE-ing in the Light, vibrating in harmony with the pure energy of the universe.

In the advanced sharing on Consciousness we share more information about the Eighth and Ninth Level of Consciousness as well as the art of *conscious communication* with the universal

Law of Eternity. At this level let us just understand that the 8th Level of Consciousness carries all eternal Karma, and the 9th Level of Consciousness is Nirvana, cessation of suffering. Once we get past the area of all questions answered, all doubts banished, we can begin to work on becoming Sages but in these meditations we are simply learning stress reduction and communication with our inner self, which with practice, leads to wisdom and enlightenment.

Meditation with practice is about Being In the Moment, it is not about shutting down the Mind, it is not about discarding our thoughts, it is about trust, realization and ability to go anywhere, anytime. I want to share with you a Quote from *Jonathan Livingston Seagull, by Richard Bach.* He has recently died and gone to Heaven only to discover there is no such place. Jonathan says to his Guide Teacher, "Chiang, this world isn't heaven at all, is it?" The Elder smiled in the moonlight. "You are learning again, Jonathan. Heaven is not a place, and it is not a time. Heaven is being perfect. You will begin to touch heaven, Jonathan in the moment you touch perfect speed. And that isn't flying a thousand miles an hour, or a million, or flying at the speed of light.

Because any number is a limit, and perfection doesn't have limits. Perfect speed is Being there." What Buddhists call the *World of Blissful Realization* is harmony at the 7th Level of Consciousness.

In our meditation we are learning that mediation is about our *vital life force* of energy. It is not about

19

using our will power, rather it is about acceptance listening to our miracle mind, then letting go!

Deep Meditative Joy offers us an opportunity to witness the sounds of silence by becoming aware we are not alone or separate from all that is. In order to be still we need to contemplate on the physics of our *vital life energy force,* the aura that surrounds all entities of life including the energy we put forth in our breathing, eating, sleeping, meditating. We are speaking here of the environment surrounding natural energy force of all phenomena. This is very spiritual, as we are reminded we are spiritual Beings on a human journey; not human beings looking for a meditative experience. One of our first Joys then is to acknowledge that we are never alone. This can be a very difficult concept to fathom when we think of self, when we articulate how hard we work at life. When we are knocked down by someone or something and we wish we were left alone. How does One dwell in the silence? The second point of Deep Meditative Joy comes from our preparation: a combination of the secret deep breath, our body scan, physically getting ready and our meditation space. This we call the *Meditation of a Thousand Ways.*

THE HINDRANCES - PART TWO

We are again reminded that we are beginning to see Meditation as a balance of Awareness, Concentration and vital Energy. When beginners start to meditate it becomes clear that everything is changing moment to moment, as the mind races from place to place like a ping pong ball in action.

Our thought patterns change and challenge, the body shifts and demands attention, we find it hard to be still, energized and concentrated. We call this our Hindrances. But because this practice is about Deep Meditative JOY, we try and rid our bodily stress before going into meditation. Again we are reminded to realize our meditations will be appropriate to the mood or condition we are in at the moment of practice. Our disposition will be determined by our posture affecting our spinal chakras, *Kundalini* nervous energy force [more about this later.]

Contemplation is made easier with non desire. So we don't try and force anything in meditation, we simply go along for the ride. It is much better not to try "will power," we do not use force, rather high meditation comes naturally from won't power. Our meditative suggestions are made without conscious effort if they are to be effective. The main point is that one practices every day, regardless of the kind of day One has had.

As we have shared, at first when we begin meditation it is normal for the body and mind to witness a settling in as the body goes through settling. As we get settled, we want to twitch, move, get up, change positions. Don't worry about these kinks with practice we will learn to **BE Still**, to ignore the itch that we want to scratch, to move our leg just a little. This then brings us to our *Body Scan, Posture and Breath!* The position we want to be in regardless of which of the Seven Classic types of Meditation we wish to practice is one of comfort and ease. We get away from weight and bulk of the body; to light and energy consciousness so the nervous energy that flows up through the body can attain its goal.

This is called *Kundalini* Yoga Meditation. Kundalini simply means flowing through, not getting rid of, it is about energy exchange, the transcendental release of Ego. So, naturally we want to be comfortable to attain this. Therefore we stretch, relax our muscles, and practice the art of breath exchange, before meditating. When it comes to *Awareness Meditation*, whether sitting or walking, we want to relax and breath with purpose.

OUR NERVOUS ENERGY SYSTEM

The next part of our warm up exercise before approaching "Deep Meditative Joy" is to get in touch with the physical *ganglia* nets that hold our sympathetic nervous system in place, our body's other half. We want to get in touch with the multi billion cell-u-lar community within our beautiful body. We want to feel our feet, liver, heart, navel and wet mass of brain matter. This is known as *Vispanna* Insight or *Mindfulness Meditation*.

BODY HEALING - AN EXERCISE

With the first body scan we simply released the new cellular oxygen to the various individual parts of the body. Now, as we breath in through our nostrils, we take this meditative exercise a further step. As before we breathe in- the *Vital Life Energy* in the lungs energizing it, holding the intake of oxygen, in this step we see and feel where our body needs restoration, renewal and with a real burst we blow out through our mouth and send the new oxygenated energy to that part of the body which needs our help in healing. Breathing in, holding, sending vital energy. Inhaling, holding, sending, exhaling, holding, Inhaling, holding, sending, Exhaling, holding, sending, circling the upper body and neck, feel the cranium fluids in the brain. Now, lightly shake the arms, hands, fingers, shoulders. This is a pathway to vital health. Breath again back to the chest, meeting at the solar plexus or mid-brain which is about two inches above the belly button protected at the bottom of the chest cavity. We are empowered with our miraculous bodies to stay younger, to assist in a healthful body, mind and spirit through our daily meditations. We need to exercise! Feel free to rest after this exercise!

There is a constant balance between the physical body and the sympathetic nervous signaling part of our body that moves our feet, hand, heart, gives us a headache, causes tension fills us with peaceful means. Science now agrees that all disease is cellular disease, whether that is heart disease, a form of cancer or a common cold. It is cellular disease connected to the sympathetic nervous system. Being in touch with the various parts of our body through these breathing and bodily meditative exercises we fuse with the universal energy power allowing for excellent meditation practice and results.

We are talking here of the passion of the spiritual energy flowing within individual karmic energy, in mutual possession with the universal mystic Law.

This is where we go with the advanced Buddhist Meditation studies and practice. For now, let us simply realize that if the rooms of our body are the light fixtures, then our sympathetic nervous systems are the various light bulbs. Understand, breathing exercises do not assist us in meditation, but bring balance to the body, allowing our consciousness to move freely with no disturbances from irregular breathing or mind wandering. There are many good books on breathing techniques, you may wish to do further research in this area, in support of your physical, mental and spiritual Health and meditative practice.

Concentrated, consistent Meditation brings the Five Desired Powers: Empathy, Compassionate Power, Mindfulness beyond mind, Realization beyond Learning, and the Sounds of Silence. We are going to experience this with our practice this evening. Regular Meditation has the power of greatly reducing stress, finding mindfulness, bringing peace and tranquillity.

SCIENCE AND THE UNIVERSAL LAW

Meditative breathing assists us to rid the left brain of distractions, so our creative quiet right brain meditative side can take over. In the silence do not worry if it takes awhile to settle down. The first ten minutes may seem like forever. We relax as we settle, we ponder thoughts running through, we seek meditative answers. We go to places we have never been, trusting in the mystic universal Law of Light and Energy.

Having set up our bodies and energy flows, with our backs straight, our head held high, we begin our Silent Meditation with a few words of appreciation for what we are about to witness. You may use whatever words move you, then silently let Go, and go where the Deep Meditative JOY takes You. We want to connect our power source [energy], to the body source, to join in perfect harmony with the universal mystic Law of energy and light.

We do this by our combination of breathing, relaxing the body parts and hosting *conscious communication* with the universal Law. With practice we do this naturally and without great effort within our meditative practice. Buddhists and Yogins for thousands of years have known that matter and energy are interchangeable. This is a **Master Key** to conscious communication with the universal eternal Law. This is the key that opens brightly into the Light. Be serene in the Oneness that all doubt may vanish. When the mind is elsewhere, ten thousand interruptions can offer no offence. Beyond the body, beyond the mind is eternity. Let go of the clinging, let go the emotions do not be influenced by externals. Seek to be All that is within, listening beyond listening, be endowed with power, fearlessness, concentration and dwell in the boundless eternal energy.

VISUALIZATION - AN EXERCISE

For this Meditation we practice in reaching for Deep Meditative JOY. Know that wisdom is not enough. We need to practice on a consistent, regular basis, easy to begin. Difficult to continue! For this

Awareness Meditation, I would like to suggest Four [4] options for One Point Visualization:

1] We pick a problem we wish solved. We let our mind work though all its functions. Then, having communicated these thoughts to the universe, we let go of all thought and enter the silence. If the mind comes back for more interruptions that is okay let them come, then go back to the breath and get back into the silence. As the answers come in this meditation trust it and feel the JOY.

2] We bring back a Person, Place or Event that has brought us much happiness. We go back there in our mind and visit again, seeing, feeling, hearing, smelling, listening, sharing, then go into the silence to feel *Deep Meditative JOY*

3] If there is something we want to forgive ourselves for, visit this in full detail. We don't worry if we get emotional, we let it happen as part of meditative letting go, then simply release this energy to the universe and go into the silence. There maybe several steps in this process but just let it happen, let the blame go, let it become JOY.

4] How about letting Love Flow. Love is about natural JOY. We have done our meditative breathing, we have stretched the body, we are comfortable. Now we can go think about Love, what does it mean to us, how much of it do we have, how much can we give? Love grows when we contemplate on the happiness of others. We all want to be loved just as others want to be loved for who they are. So we stretch our mind around the World of Love and see where it takes us. For surely here we will find Deep Joy.

It's Still About You

The important thing in practising meditation is not to worry about the mental state we are in or the length of time we are going to practice, or whether we are doing it correctly or not; we *just do it*. The only requirement is simple sincerity, as we achieve empowerment and bliss!

We are reminded then, it is important that we be washed and clean. That we settle ourselves, taking a few moments to practice the meditative holding breath, breathing in and out with the rhythm of our heart-beat as we prepare to enjoy our empowerment and communication with the *universal mystic Law of Eternity*.

All our meditation energy goes out into the universe being heard and responded to. Naturally, we want a clean place, a respectful place to practice. We make sure others respect our energy, our environmental spiritual space. We stay away from people, places and events that do not respect our learning, realization and wisdom!

We know we have achieved an enlightened moment when we enter a blissful state of mind and body that carries the self through to a higher world of consciousness. This is most difficult to explain with words, it being a state we *Realize*, a gift to our Inner Self.

We treat our meditation time with the same attitude as if one of our most cherished, loved family members or friend were coming to visit us this day, at this very moment. Then, even if we are in a bad state of mind, our energy flow will alter as we accept the goodness of friendship, love and true self.

It is important to understand, in meditating we may make conscious communication with all that is, past, present and future, beyond our common understanding. So we accept with gratitude that all our meditative efforts are virtuous acts of an individual offering and will bring benefit, fortune and merit into our life. We meditate with concentration with high self esteem, which leads to the contemplative mind. We go places beyond words. We will witness answers to questions we were afraid to ask. We will solve problems of long standing. We will find harmony and peace in our BE-ing. However, like any new task this takes time. It is different for each of us depending on our karma. Well done, well done!

What Do You See, What Do You Hear

Meditation Is An Offering

Balance

Consciousness Volition - Energy Force

Revisiting Posture & Breath

InSight Meditation Exercises

Meditation Guide To Peaceful Means

Meditation, "is like melting ice into water, it is not something apart and does not come from elsewhere. All is contained in a single moment of mind." Tien. Tai Chi'I

What Do You Hear...   What Do You See...

*"It is when I meditate that I can find
the universe that's locked beyond my
mind" Sebastian Temple*

All meditation comes from the ancient art of Yoga in the East. In our day and age Meditation means many different things to each of us. Certainly for half a century now, in North America, meditation is realized and has proven to be a method of release from tension, a method to reduce heart and mind stress. Our body is the temple, our mind the miracle and meditation the diamond jewel within. This is what we are sharing and practicing, giving us an opportunity to practice the discipline of regular spiritual meditation as well as generic meditation. I hope we can realize the premise that meditation is a spiritual exercise of the body, mind and spirit, whatever our faith or understanding of a higher power that many in the West choose to call God.

InSight life really is about IN-Sight. What we perceive, what we hear, what we see for this insight will be our guide to health, happiness and prosperity or not! Life is a journey of lessons in this our "saha" world, the world of endurance. Here is what the Buddha has to say about InSight. From Chapter Two of our *Lotus Sutra*, "the Buddha's, the World-Honoured Ones, appear in the worlds in order to cause all living beings to open the gate to the insight of the Buddha, and to cause them to purify themselves." They appear in the worlds in order to show the insight of the Buddha to all living beings. They appear in the worlds in order to cause all living beings to obtain the insight of the Buddha. They appear in the worlds in order to cause all living beings to enter the Way to the insight of the Buddha.

Although there are examples of specific Buddhist meditation practice, all the examples given are open to the more generic meditative practice. We know the historical Buddha practiced Yoga Meditation throughout his life as there was no Buddhist practice before the Buddha taught the way of the Buddha teachings. The Buddha-way continues to use meditation on the freeway to wisdom, less stress and enlightenment.

We are sharing Three Main Pathways of Meditation that will give us the tools for whatever purpose brings us together at this time. I began Yogic Meditations in the 1970's and then specific Buddhist Meditations in the 1980's and have lived in the land of peaceful means "go shi annon" for the most part ever since. This is called actual proof of practice. Meditation results in the here and Now.

Meditation Is An Offering

Meditation teaches us layers of concentration and contemplation that lead us beyond the six senses to the seventh level of consciousness; which docs several things. Firstly it reduces a cluttered and often too busy mind, helps with good health by regulating our breathe, raises awareness, provides us with insight. It has been scientifically proven to reduce stress, assist with problem solving and brings moments of bliss far beyond words. Not a bad habit or practice we might conclude.

"Hearing is about seeing. Seeing is about opening the mind, as well as our eyes!"
TMHenry

All Meditation is an offering. Hearing is about seeing, feeling, listening, in the emotion of empathy. In this Meditation, with practice, we naturally reach an awareness of all that goes on around us. Mindfulness Meditation is about leaving off the chatter of our miracle mind and focusing on the *Moment of Now*. It is the kind of training a police officer receives in learning to pay attention to all details of what's going down quickly and efficiently. All meditation is about stress reduction and empowerment through exercise and experience.

This Insight Meditation is about self growth, about letting go, about acceptance. It is about Mindfulness and No Mind, it is about Emptyness and Fullness. It is about nothing and everything.

FISHING NET - AN EXERCISE

In this Meditation I want you to think about a *Fishing Net*. I want you to concentrate on what you see, meditating for two to three minutes. Now, how many of you saw a Spider Web, for we are told, this is where the idea for the fishing net comes from, in relationship with the principle of catching things. Life is about perception and mistakes leading to success.

As noted earlier, meditation is about going anywhere, anytime, it is about an open mind to what may appear. Pick a flower, a leaf on a tree, a universal star on a bright night. With consistent practice we will witness proof that meditation, is not about the teacher, it is about the experience. With practice it will take us places that sit in front of our eyes yet, we are too busy to see. The main focus at the moment is about our internal compass. It is about humility and trust found. It is about paying attention, focusing and visualizing beyond the stress and everyday noise that surround us.

IT IS ABOUT BALANCE

As we are beginning to see, Meditation is a balance of awareness, concentration and energy. When we start to meditate it becomes clear that everything is changing, moment to moment, as the mind races from place to place like a ping pong ball in action. Our thought patterns change and challenge, the body shifts and demands attention, we find it hard to be still, energized and concentrated. We call these our body hindrances.

Therefore, it is important to realize our meditations will be appropriate to the mood or condition we are in at the moment of practice. Our disposition will be determined by our posture affecting our Chakras and *Kundalini* or nervous energy force. They depend on our approach or method, our attitude of desire or non desire. It is much better not to try Will Power, we do not use force, rather high meditation comes naturally from Won't Power. Your meditative suggestions must be made without conscious effort if they are to be effective. The main point is that we practice every day, regardless of the kind of day we have had. We meditate through frustration or anger, we meditate through sadness or sorrow, meditating in joy and happiness. Always we meditate with acceptance and coming realization.

CONSCIOUSNESS VOLITION, ENERGY FORCE

To reach for Light, energy, life force, and One's Truth, the Worlds are *Learning and Realization* natural to all Beings on the pathway of self-realization, wisdom and enlightenment. There is within the universal energy field of our Being a need to keep reaching, a natural desire for more, thereby pursuing our earthly desires with a balanced passion in a healthy manner that is right and good.

Beyond the Five Senses of our Objective Consciousness: seeing, hearing, feeling, tasting, smelling, and the Sixth Sense of Volition. Volition allows us to see, hear, feel, taste, touch, smell. We hold in our Subjective Mind: the subconscious mind that holds our habits, reasoning, will power, imagination and eternal memory.

In our *Meditations* we desire to achieve a natural Seventh Level of Consciousness. What Buddhists call the World of Realization, the start of which we recognize as a simple profound moment of Ahh, a state of Energy Awareness. This touches our deep intuition, our true soul-mate. Beyond the Seventh Level is the Eighth all important

Alaya- Consciousness and the Ninth never ending Nirvana Light consciousness; in two formats, nirvana with reside, and nirvana without reside.

As we approach *Meditation* we should not get discouraged when we do not get the results we are immediately seeking. Meditation takes much practice. We are renewing habits of the subconscious mind, we are multi-tasking in the sense that we are trying to realize some subjective factors that lead to objective mindfulness.

With practice we do not try at these things, they just happen naturally. We just know, we just do, we appreciate the peace and serenity our Meditation brings. With practice we find realization, joy, blissfulness, beyond what humble words can simply express. However, it takes discipline, does not come easily for everyone and is dependent on One's individual karma.

This whole area of Consciousness is serious knowledge and One can spend many years studying and relating to the wonders of the Conscious Being of our past, present and future existence. Meditation is one method of becoming closer to our Consciousness by reaching out beyond the physical reaching for One's Spiritual Health.

I would like to share a quote from The Prophet by *Kahlil Gibran*, "An old priest said, Speak to us of Religion. And he said: Is not religion all deeds and all reflection, and that which is neither deed nor reflection, but a wonder and a surprise ever springing in soul, even while the hands hew the stone or tend the loom? Your daily life is your temple and your religion." Or, as the Buddha shared: "No affairs of life or work are in any way different from the ultimate reality." The Meditation point in these statements is that we are not separate from anything.

THE MUFFIN - AN EXERCISE

When we want to practice insight meditation it is with wonder and surprise that we look at a Muffin and see the sun and rain feeding the field of wheat, and the man on the tractor cutting the wheat, and the trucks and their drivers transporting the raw wheat, and the manufacturing plants packaging the wheat, and the bakeries adding the ingredients, and where did all those ingredients come from and how many people where involved, and how many miles did it travel to get to market? Now that it is before me, what do I see? How is the texture, the colour, the flavour, the nutrients, the taste of this humble healthy muffin? How aware of all that is, am I, in this moment of concentration and meditation? How connected am I?

Being in the mind set of IN-Sight we are not in the mind set of stress, worrying about the children, our job, our business, our partners in life, our economic situation; we are learning to live just in the moment of *Being Here*.

Revisiting Posture & Breath - Vital Life Force Breath

At first when we begin meditation practice it is normal for the body and mind to witness a settling in, when the body goes through mind games and positioning pain. As we get settled, we want to twitch, move, get up, change positions. These are the Hindrances we mentioned earlier. Don't worry about these kinks. With practice we learn to BE Still, to ignore the itch that we want to scratch, to move our leg just a little. This then brings us to *Posture and Breath!* When it comes to posture there are Meditation courses that charge hundreds and even thousands of dollars and practice all kinds of different mudras and postures. It is just posturing for money. The position you want to be in regardless of whether you are doing *Silent Meditation, Walking Meditation or Sound Meditation* is one of comfort and ease, so you can get away from weight and bulk, to light and energy. Part of which is a straight back, so the nervous energy that flows through the body can attain its goal. This is known as our *Kundalini* energy flow. Kundalini simply means flowing through, it is about energy exchange, the transcendental release of Ego. Meditation readiness means we want to be comfortable so a good stretch, a relaxing of the muscles is a good start before all meditation, as is controlled breath!

We are reminded that there are Four parts of every breath we take. Inflowing - Energy flowing or Kundalini - Outflowing and Energy flowing. Earlier we studied and practiced the secret of the Yoga's that it is the holding of the breath that spreads the prana or vital Life Energy of Health. When we practice this deep meditative breath then the body and mind hindrances for the most part work themselves out before we begin our actual meditation. In fact this is as far as some meditation practices go, just watching and counting the breath, this is a fine practice for beginners.

Going back to the breath, we set up our *Vital Life Energy Breath* with a simple 6-3-6-3, Counting Six In, Three Hold, Six Out, Three Hold, Six In, Three Hold, Six Out, Three Hold, Six times. With practice we may wish to increase this to a natural 8-4-8-4, or even 10–5-10-5, depending on our metabolism, sending a healthful first step of meditation throughout the body as we energize in order to realize. It is not about the counting, but in realizing the whole body breath.

The wisdom here is in the *"Kundalini Energy Flow, or vital life force."* The breathing In and Out only provides partial Health care for the body. The holding or half pause, between breathes is the hidden method of yogic practice, as it increases flow of energy to all parts of the body. When we see someone in very good health into their eighties and nineties one of the main reasons is correct breathing whether they are aware of it or not.

Yet we come to understand breathing exercises are not actual meditation. They bring balance to the body, allowing our consciousness to move freely with no disturbances from irregular breathing or mind wandering. There are many good books on breathing techniques. You may wish to do further research in this area in support of your physical, mental and spiritual health and meditative practice.

So, go ahead now, take a few minutes and practice this breathing, become comfortable as the Vital Energy Force exhales the carbon dioxide and brings in new oxygen, Breathing in, holding, the vital energy automatically moving to those parts of the body that need it. Inhaling, holding, sending, exhaling, holding, Inhaling, holding, sending, Exhaling, holding, sending, relaxing, counting the breaths, or simply watching the intake, pause, exhale and pause, before the next breath.

There is a constant balance between the physical body and the sympathetic nervous system of our body that moves our feet, hands, heart, gives us a headache, causes tension, fills us with peaceful means. Science now agrees that all disease is cell disease, whether it is heart disease, a form of cancer or a common cold. It is cellular disease connected to the sympathetic nervous system. Being in touch with the various parts of our body through these breathing exercises and bodily meditative exercises we fuse with the universal energy power allowing for excellent meditation practice and results.

We are talking here of the passion of the spiritual energy flowing within individual karmic energy, in mutual possession with the universal mystic Law. This is where we go with the advanced Buddist Meditation studies and practice. For now, let us simply realize that if the rooms of our body are the light fixtures, then our sympathetic nervous systems are the various light bulbs.

We are reminded that all Meditation is a balance of awareness, concentration and energy. Meditation has the power of mindfulness, bringing peace and tranquillity. We are reminded a simple warmup exercise before beginning meditation is all we need. Stretch the ankles, swing the arms around, roll the neck releasing the stress that separates the spinal column, from the brain stem. Breathing deeply for two to three minutes, we are ready, for some InSight meditative practice.

Having stretched the body, breathing in harmony we are now introduced to various subjects for us to concentrate on, leading us to a contemplate mind, dwelling in the silence, what do we hear, what do we see?.

> *"Never lose an opportunity to realize*
> *the beauty in all things, beauty is the*
> *handwriting of life" HL*

MEDITATION ON BEAUTY - Ten to Twenty Minutes

- We think back to a beautiful memory, a flower, a hug, an ocean wave, a scene in the forest
- We re-create that scene part by part, piece by piece, in our master minds eye

- Its colour, feel the majesty, bring past into present
- We wrap our energy aura in this journey, feeling this beautiful experience once again
- Feel the handwriting of love within, breathe in the beauty
- Beauty everywhere in life and death, go now with this moment

We Enter Silent Meditation

Then We Share Our Active Meditation Application

- Over the next week we find a particle of beauty; a flower, a bird's wingtip, a refraction of sunlight
- We focus our attention on all the hundreds of details surrounding this beautiful One instant
- Seeing the colour, softness, brightness, coolness, warmth, texture of this very moment
- We fill our self with Beauty in the here and now, developing our Seventh level of consciousness.

MEDITATION ON PATIENCE - Ten to Twenty Minutes

"The principle part of faith is patience"
George Macdonald

- How often are we impatient, how often do we doubt
- What is so important
- Does impatience come from self doubt, do we not believe we are connected to all that is
- We are whole, seeking our Oneness in patience is good and worthy

- We all have the potential to achieve wisdom and enlightenment
- Now is the time to be quiet and patient, leave work and worry for another day
- We read, study, reflect on forgiveness of personal faults, resolving to grow
- Daily with patience, cast off doubt, believe in our dreams, make our visions bright.
- Contemplate our Oneness, understand we are evolving according to our karmic efforts in this lifetime
- Evolving our truest self-nature, being patient with self and others

We Enter Silent Meditation

Then We Share Our Active Meditation Application

In one of the Buddha's teachings, the Fugen Sutra shares with us: "If you wish to make amends, performing Sange, which is to acknowledge ones's faults, misdeeds, wrongful actions, seeking to expiate the negative karma associated with such actions, taking control of One's inner Being, sit upright and meditate on the true entity of life, and all your offenses will vanish like frost and dewdrops in the sunlight of enlightened wisdom." Let us put this into perspective as we meditate on Patience.

MEDITATION ON SPIRITUAL LIGHT - Ten to Twenty Minutes

> *"The Buddha-nature within every person is our spiritual reality allowing us to develop and use our fullest human powers"* HL

- What is my understanding of Love, how many kinds are there, what are my expectations
- What does it mean to me, do I need to develop a better realization of the function of Love
- What does non attachment mean to me
- May the Light that shines in all ten directions grant me knowledge and realization that I may Find Right Speech, Right Thought, Discover Right Motivation, take Right Action, that my truest self may prosper, inviting perfect health, empowering me to help myself and others, to be loving to let go of anger, to be peaceful, Let me BE Mindful of the Spiritual Light of wisdom, love and non-attachment

We Enter Silent Meditation

Then We Share Our Active Meditation Application

- Over the next week we pick someone to directly show our love to
- We focus our mind on sharing this moment in a dynamic way
- We love life within spiritual Light, happiness through mindfulness

CLOUD MEDITATION

- Imagine a Cloud being born, coming into BE-ing
- Where was it before it became a cloud, was born as a cloud
- What kind of cloud do we see, how big is it, how small, how light
- Does it fill the sky... or is it just a puff of a cloud
- Is the wind moving the clouds quickly or slowly...
- What do I see..... what do I hear............

Be mindful of who you are now..... ask yourself where was I before I came into BE-ing, how do I see the inter-dependent reality of my body, mind and spirit; do I believe I have a soul, if so where does it reside, will it die when I do

How does a cloud, a rain drop, a sunny day relate to my BE-ing
What does cultivating the mind mean to me

We Enter Silent Meditation

Then We Share Our Active Meditation Application

- In the coming week go for a walk and look up into the sky
- What do you see.... stop and meditate on what you see
- What thoughts come into your Walking Meditation
- Get that Spiritual Diary out and write down your thoughts

ENLIGHTENING MEDITATION

See this Day, realize it's length of light and darkness
What does this day offer, how much of nature will
I be able to share
Meditate on the past five years, where was I, how
was I
See into the future, where do I want to be, how will
I get there

We Enter Silent Meditation

Then We Share Our Active Meditation Application

- In the coming week, daily go for a Meditation
  Walk
- Evaluate with your mindfulness, think about
  how, why, where, what, when
- Realize that by controlling the mind to see
  clearly, we gain greater control over all that is....

MEDITATION GUIDE TO PEACEFUL MEANS

The Buddhist Eightfold Pathway

Right Thought

Right Motivation

Right Action

Right Endeavor

Right Views

Right Effort

Right Meditation,

Right Contemplation

Within this pathway our meditation experience offers us major tools to expand, enhance and grow our Insight and Mindfulness.

We remember all Meditation is an offering. It is the holding of quality Self-time with consistency of practice as we attain powerful strength, quietude and bliss consciousness. Filled with self respect and purity of purpose, we help bring peaceful means to ourself and others.

We imagine birds as flights of ideas. Think of boats as rafts to cross the rivers of life's challenges, transporting our happiness, floating us to abundance. We are all given the same time, 24 hours in a day, it is our task to ask how much of each day do we choose to devote to our spiritual Health.

Walking Meditation

Several Methods

Five Reasons

Walking Method

A Buddhist Way

Nichiren Seven Step

Walking In Concentration

"All techniques are built around breath, mantra, concentration, leading to concentration that leads to contemplation as the pathway to deep meditation" HL

STOPPING AND SEEING

The developmental stages of all meditation are for the realization of inner self, thereby realizing One's temporary nature, we can work on our eternal or Buddha nature. One of the most profound methods is in allowing our Walks to become a deep meditation; whether we are walking in a park, enjoying nature at a public or personal sanctuary.

SEVERAL METHODS

Walking meditation, of course, is very different from our sitting meditation, although it includes breath, hatha yoga, and a portion of quietude that often brings gratitude for what we are observing. The first method is in the Awareness of nature by observing where we are walking. The second method is an offering done with a Seven Step, repetitive walk that includes observing the precepts, chanting and repeating a verse about the Oneness of universal all.

Going anywhere, anytime is a Buddhist phrase we often share in our Buddhist Way. Here is a good place to help us visit the higher Eighth *World of Realization*. Here we can realize one of natures most unrealized Meditations in Walking! Walking meditation is truly a method to find Oneself going anywhere, anytime! Walking meditation, is meditation in action, as we realize the ancient saying: *"no matter how long we look down the road, if we just look down the road, we will never arrive."* We must walk!

We are reminded that all Meditation should be an offering. Whether in silence, in chanting or in walking, we are given five reasons for Meditating:

1] to understand a practice that leads to wisdom and enlightenment
2] to learn how to utilize this wisdom and enlighten our lives
3] to pay a debt of gratitude to the Three Treasures for this Life
4] to work towards personal growth for Health, Happiness, Prosperity
5] to share our Spiritual Health, assisting others to find the Joy of Life

The Great Chinese Master *Tien Tai Chi"* I, explains the various methods of Walking Meditation and tells us the amount of time that Monks should spend in Walking Meditation as: "a little Daily, Seven days and Ninety days". Due to the universal Law of Cause, Karma and Effect, we come to believe that our faith, prayers, meditations, offerings are heard and must be acted upon. Therefore, we individually become active participants in making mother Earth a safer place, a place of spiritual sustain-ability and peaceful means.

The *Universally Equal* scripture says: *"when you practice meditation, the spiritual Guardian Energies are witnesses."* Meditation, then, can be a "spiritual awakening" that leads to no doubt about doctrinal theology.

With practice we begin to understand every thing we do can be a Meditation. It can take us to any place, any time as we become ONE with the mystic Law of Light and Energy that governs our universe. We are reminded here, to not become frustrated if we don't feel deep results right away, every form of meditation takes time and practice just like all other habits. Start with understanding that *Meditation is a Healthy habit!*

Going anywhere, anytime means Meditation takes on many forms, when we become aware and contemplative. From practice, awareness, insightfulness and walking moments of enlightenment can come naturally. Relaxing and letting go with our breath at ease, we become one without earthly emotion, and we will often arrive in the seventh [7th] level of consciousness, the land of Blissful BE-ing!

WALKING METHOD

Sometimes we are just in a rush and we are going places quickly. Even so, we may be blessed when we are walking with Right Attitude, to see something spectacular in our pathway, a blessing for the moment, a blessing for this day!

If one lives in the city, he or she can chose a lovely park walkway, walking back and forth or walking in a circle. Our choice, whichever we feel brings more peaceful results. The reality is meditation is a connection of provisional mind with universal

Mind. The result dependent largely on practice, the habit calming. *Just twenty minutes a day, so simple, so difficult.* If we are fortunate we will have a Sangha with Meditation Walkways, where we can practice anytime. Such as at the Nichiren Peace Center, here on Vancouver Island, in the Cowichan Valley. Other times we take our practice in any public place, as we walk for our Health, Happiness and Prosperity.

A Buddhist Way

Seeing a thousand things is the Buddhist way. How often have we been re-reading a book and think, when did they add this section or paragraph? Walking meditation is magic because everything changes with the seasons and the weather. As Buddhists, we can begin our Meditation by Chanting the Infinite Title of the Lotus Sutra, making our Opening Invocation, asking the heavenly *Guardian Energies* to hear and be with us in the here and Now. Quietly turn to the Buddha's of the Ten Directions, stretch and relax the body, follow our breath In/Hold/Out/Hold ten times, Join our palms and begin to Walk. During a Walking Meditation the various exercises may include: counting the breaths, chanting to calm the mind, becoming aware of each step then Stopping and Seeing, as Tien Tai so beautifully shares.

This method is to slowly walk until you are moved to stop. Observing all around you; what do you see, what do you hear, how are the senses attuned to the moment. We observe silently, then perhaps write a few notes in our *Meditation Diary* for expanded meditation later.

In our outdoor practice we can make our *Heaven and Earth* offering: *"The Earth and the Heavens are One, I AM One"* walking for a ways, then do a little chanting while we walk until we get to a Meditation Bench or nature stops us with a moment of beauty and realization. It may be a sunrise, a sunset, the warmth of the day. We simply become alive and aware, what do you see, hear, observe, feel? The great Chinese Master Teacher/Messenger, Tien Tai Chi'I [538 - 597 c.e.] called this *Stopping and Seeing*. It can be very profound and take us to magical places.

NICHIREN SEVEN STEP: *A Specific Walking Meditation*

As an offering, the Buddhist Sage Nichiren's Seven step specific walking meditation is a joy and a declaration that we understand... the Eternity of Life! With each step as a syllable one chants the Infinite Title of the Lotus Sutra, *Na Mu Myo Ho Ren Ge Kyo*, then stopping we say: *"The Earth and the Heavens Are One, I AM One."* This comes from the famous story of the High Braham Priests challenging the Buddha *Gautama Shakyamuni* asking who he thought he was to suggest that the Indian Caste system was unjust. In response he placed his hands downward and is said to have stated "the earth is my witness." Also, in his early teachings he taught about *interdependent origination,* which later *Nagrajuna* explained as the Buddhist concept of "Oneness."

We point downward towards Earth palms of hands open saying "the Earth" then rising the arms and joining our hands, upwards above the head saying "and the Heaven's are One," then bringing our hands down to our Heart Shakra, saying I AM One; completing the fusion of joining our Universal Law with our Heart-Minds!

Method: walking and stopping we repeat the offerings, walking in a circle or back and forth, in the following manner: *Na-Mu* – first step forward, second foot comes stopping alongside the first, we stop a second until finishing the Mu particle, moving forward now with each step, *Myo-Ho-Ren-ge -Kyo,* ending with feet together, we stop and chant: *"The Earth and the Heavens Are One, I AM One."* With this method of walking and offering we can walk for a short distance or a long one, the calming and clarity of mind soon begins to help us become very aware of all that surrounds us.

WALKING AWARENESS - BEAUTY EVERYWHERE

Meditation is the joining of spirit, mind and body. It takes serious practice. For some the journey is long and difficult. Yet in reality for most it is only a matter of discipline until meditation becomes a *habit of beauty and wonder.* There are three levels of concentration: beginning, middle and deep. These are the abodes of concentration and the key to realizing each is to keep coming back to our breath, our mindful calming by silent chanting, and our meditation on one point of concentration at a time. In time we will naturally move into middle concentration and finally into deep concentration which becomes contemplative and blissful.

Perhaps in our *Walking Meditation* we will want to meditate on one of the Six Perfections or practices: Alms Giving, Morality, Patience, Perseverance, Energy, Wisdom. Meditate in the Moment - pick one of the perfections of practice, on seeking deep InSight. We walk for awhile we find a bench stop and meditate there until we feel it is time to walk again.

Perhaps we will want to mediate on specific subjects such as: *bliss, joy, mindfulness, insightfulness, equality.* We use Oneness meditation on the profound meaning of these words, one at a time over and over again until we are happy with the results, then, move on to the next subject, reaching for insightfulness. There is so much we can meditate on as we reach towards the *Eighth World of Realization!*

In our *Walking Meditation* we are reminded that everything is connected, nothing is truly independent. Walking and meditating are joined, seeing and hearing are joined, mountains and streams, river beds and oceans, trees, plants and animals, including humans, all a part of our eternal Buddha nature. Life giving worms, squirrels, birds of all forms, the grasses, trees, plants are all apart of the cycle of what we call life and death.

In reality, all are forms of the constant changing fusion of Light and Energy, that which we call the original Buddha nature. This makes it easier for lay people to understand, as we are not Quantum

Physic Scientists. Our Spiritual Meditations are Quantum Physics in Action. How great this is!

As it is shared, to seek enlightenment, we chop wood, harvest vegetables, carry water; having found enlightenment, we chop wood, harvest vegetables, carry water. All are interconnected to a beginning, a middle and an ending. Then we repeat the cycle. Walk now in Peace, meditate with *Awareness and InSight*, this is the pathway to Health and a life of indestructible Happiness.

Let's go now for a Walk finding beauty everywhere, then come back and reflect: what did we see, what did we hear, what did we touch, what did we smell, what and who did we listen to?

Sound Meditation

Mantra As A Way of Meditation

My Heart Soul Mantra

Meditation As Medicine

More About Our Nervous System

Sound Practice - Spiritual Mantras

"The performance of repetitive chanting represents the key significance in my ability to correctly resolve each and every problem that I encounter, at all times and in all places."

Nikken Shonin

SESSION FIVE   HEART - SOUL MEDITATION

SOUND MEDITATION

First step is exercising the body in preparation for meditation. Second step to begin meditation is by counting or watching the breath. Clear away the mind and body hindrances; following our breath, a good beginning toward concentration that lead us to contemplation. As we develop Right Mindfulness.

The next step in calming the Mind is to quietly or silently chant a Mantra, that is a short few lines or words that have meaning for You. This master key to Right Meditation is the ability to utilize a single short phrase of words over and over. When the mind wanders, quietly chant over and over any key word or phrase until you fall into mindfulness not even aware that you are no longer chanting, having entered the Meditation Zone.

A great mantra is the Infinite Title of the **Lotus Sutra**: "NAM MYOHO RENGE KYO" A simple translation is: *I take refuge in the Buddha, to quiet my mind, to understand reality, to be at peace within*. Do not grasp or reach for it, just BE. It is not about will power, it is about won't power. Our Buddha nature already IS. Stay Right Here in the moment and meditate on the One Point of the Mantra. All is the realm of reality, stay in the sound that resides within. With daily meditation we develop Right Speech, Right Thought; are more empowered to take Right Action bringing more Health, Happiness and Prosperity into our life. Mantra repetition helps control the mind, the repeating of the phrase or words over and over calms the mind. One may use any phrase or words that feel Right, one can even make up their own personal mantra's, which is what I do when working with clients with serious addictions or mental issues.

The purpose of meditation is to share the Light within. The purpose of chanting is to stabilize the mind from wandering. Focus on an object of meditation that supports one's meditation. The Law of attraction within us finds the mystic, eternal Law that guides our Universe and awakens our human nature. Congratulations on your seeking Spirit.

"Sound Meditation ~
In tune with the Eternal Vibration,
chanting my mantra"

With the use of "sound meditation" One brings five of the main steps of meditation into one. Chanting forces breathing, sharpens the chakras, uses sound, has an object of respect for concentration and is done in a devotional manner. Meditation works to establish Ones *"true self"* with an indestructible strength of character enabling one to understand that life is change and temporary.

One must be strong to survive all challenges and lessons from the worlds *of Learning and Realization*. There are several kinds of sound: the noise outside, the outer hearing, the non attentive listening, There are the internal sounds of our thought patterns, which with practice leads to a controlling of the mind leading into the awareness of light and energy that moves our universe. This brings new understanding and realizations of who I AM, why I AM here, where I AM going.

As the mind concentrates on the energies of the mantra, contemplation naturally takes place. When one attains this level of knowing and attains the state of "non back sliding," One comes to understand that happiness and suffering are One and the same, that good and bad are not different, that life and death are One circle of Dharma. Meditation leads to Right Thought, Right Motivation, and Right Action. At one phase of living we are happy, at another we are sad, at another we are filled with joy, then suddenly with pain. Such are the human characteristics of life on our planet. *The Ten Worlds* as expressed in the Middle Day of the Law, by *Tien Tai Chi'I*, are in constant motion on the Dharma Wheel of Life. We call our world the *saha* or world of endurance. However, it is also said that "one glorious day on earth, is worth a thousand days in the other worlds."

MANTRA AS WAY OF MEDITATION

In our earlier Meditation Sessions we discovered Deep Meditation Joy in our Awareness and Silence. We will experience, new Insight in our What Do You Hear, What do you See session. We have discovered how the simple act of walking can be a beautiful form of meditation. We learned the "Ten Qualities of Meditation:" daily discipline, correct place [harmony] sincerity, self-respect, simplicity, non attachment or no doubt, contentment, patience, and personal realization.

At the beginning we introduced the Seven Classic Types of Meditation: Breath, Visualization, Point [chakra, kundalini energy], Sound [mantra chanting], Movement walking, Concentration and Contemplation of the eternal essence. We discussed the Three Stages of Meditation Development or *Dhyanas*, calmness, non attachment and oneness with all phenomen or, Being in the Light.

In Meditation, as in other sciences, simplicity indicates evidence of strength and stability. Taking meditation seriously we find ourselves becoming masters of our minds instead of our minds running us around in busy, stressful mode. In Quantum physics a particle is regarded as a concentration of energy. Meditation is about contemplation with and through the particles of energy of mind, body and spirit in the here and NOW. In past sessions we began development of deep silence and insight awareness. In this session we will practice the magic and energy of Sound Meditation, the sound of our beautiful voice, externally and internally.

FIVE IN ONE ~ CHANTING ~ SOUND MEDITATION

We are told in the Lotus Sutra: *"the gods beat their celestial drums, and made all kinds of music, fragrant breezes sweep away the faded flowers, while raining others of fresh beauty."* What beauty, what joy, here is a meditation for a lifetime. Now, we learn the secret of ridding the mind of meditative hindrances through a quick body scan, some warm up breathing and today through the use of sound meditation, the music of our voice. This brings Five main steps in meditation into one, which is why we call it the *Five In One Meditation*. Chanting enforces natural breathing, uses visualization, sharpens awareness, optimizes a mantra for sound, which leads to silent contemplation. Sound in a natural way raises our level of consciousness. Meditation works to establish Ones "true self" with an indestructible strength of character enabling one to understand that life is change and temporary. One must be strong to survive all challenges and lessons from the worlds of Learning and Realization. Buddhists call our world the saha or world of endurance. However, it is also said that "one glorious day on earth, is worth a thousand days in the other worlds."

MEDITATION AS MEDICINE

Before chanting, we warm up with our body stretch toes, ankles, hands, arms, neck, spine, as we do before each meditation. As we have repeated, Meditation is a balance of awareness, concentration and energy. In the beginning, the body shifts and demands attention, and we find it hard to be still, energized and concentrated. And here is where chanting is the medicine to drive away our Hindrances. How does chanting do this, take away our body and mind hindrances?

The main point is that one should practice daily, developing a powerful and empowering habit, regardless of the kind of day one has had. Soon there is Joy in chanting through frustration or anger, chanting even with sadness or sorrow, chanting with joy and happiness, chanting for health or wealth; but always chanting. This is the *Meditation of the Thousand Ways*. This Meditation brings the Five Desired Powers, empathy, understanding, compassion, mindfulness beyond mind, and eternal answers to One's quest.

VOICE

Chanting	Words and symbol formulas consisting of a short group of select words
Sound	Syllables which effect mind, body and spirit through "energy vibration"
Meditation	Has four areas of consideration
Manipura:	Power of the spoken word, the language of thought
Pingala:	Nerve Energy channel on the right side of the body
Ida:	Nerve Energy channel on the left side of the body
Susumna:	Central nervous channel of the spine

Just as complicated mathematical formulas are unreadable to the untrained mind, so are the secrets revealed in the spiritual aspects of "*Sound Meditation.*" Chanting sets up electric-magnetic fields of energy creating an aura of voice, protection and power. Naturally, we will chant according to our present life condition, be that anger, stress, relaxed, in harmony or out of harmony, in rhythm with our heart beat and mind waves. Chanting in *Sound Meditation* has an effect on the human body, mind and spirit.

Meditation is always a personal offering, empowering us to find spiritual and personal growth, enabling us to make *"conscious communication"* with the infinite eternal Law, some choose to call God, others understand it is simply eternity at work in our universe.

Chanting is made up of three phases:

> 1] the sound of the word or words
> > 2] the motivation or sense of purpose
> > > 3] the offering and manifestation

Chanting is, therefore, not about just the words; the force is in their audible pronunciation which produces vibration. We must take care to never allow our words, thoughts and actions to deteriorate into disrespect. Our words, voice, speech and emotions work together. ***Our universe is made up of pure energy.*** Buddhist's tap into this energy force using various forms of meditation including silence, insightful awareness and music or sound Meditation. Slowing down the mind is vital! This is why we prepare with our breath and stretching exercise. In time our discipline, relaxation and letting go leads us to the higher levels of consciousness and Realization.

More About Our Nervous System

Our body system is divided into three main parts: 1] central nervous system within the brain and spinal cord 2] peripheral nervous system, including the *receptor* and the *afferent* electro- magnetic impulses of the mind, 3] a vital life force, the *spiritual* or Kundalini energy. We average about 67,000 thoughts everyday, and there are 72,000 nerve passages throughout our body.

Herein, lies *personal empowerment*. With practice of Sound Meditation, the power of chanting energizes, protects, and responds to One's earthly desires, stabilizes the mind and functions to bring peaceful means, whether walking or meditating in a sacred space. At the higher levels of consciousness we achieve a feeling beyond words. With practice One achieves *"mantra consciousness"* the blissful harmony coming from the sound of your beautiful voice, the harmonious flow of nervous energy vibrating within our body. In chanting we are trying to merge the words and our consciousness into their transcendental origin. "One uses the short phrases or mantras to reveal the Word, in *"conscious communication" with eternity"*. We are raising our levels of light and consciousness providing health's mega vitamins and minerals. Mantra chanting is a healthy powerful practice and mental empowerment.

Think of our Meditation practice as that of climbing a mountain, there are various meditation practices to take us to the top, the paths seem to lead into various locations we must keep seeking until we find actual proof that pathway we are following to the top of the mountain leads us to harmony and peaceful means. Explore, discover, research, seek out various teachings. Practice and come to your own wonderful World of Realization. The discipline is subtle, but beyond the discipline is joy and insightfulness far beyond words of expression. There are three kinds of truth, the truth as I see it, the truth as others see it and the truthful realization of mutual understanding. Meditating assists us to listen fully and to discover deeper meanings in the people, places and events that go on in our life.

The secret wisdom here is in the *"Energy Flow, or vital life force."* The breathing In and Out only provides partial Health care for the body. The holding period between breathe is a secret of the ages as it increases flow of energy to all parts of the body. When you see someone in very good health into their eighties and nineties one of the main reasons for their balance is correct breathing whether they are aware of it or not. We understand breathing exercises are not actual in meditation, but lead us to mindfulness, bring balance to the body, allow our consciousness to move freely with no disturbances from irregular breathing or mind wandering. There are many good books on breathing techniques, you may wish to do further research in this area in support of your physical, mental and spiritual Health and meditative practice.

Let's review and practice some mantras, the words and symbol formulas consisting of a short group selected words or syllables which affect the mind, body and spirit through *"conscious energy vibration"* Mantras have no beginning and no ending, they respectively flow in and out with the breath of our heart beat.

A primary Word is Nadis which is the internal symmetry of conscious sound, the plexis vibrations producing the mantra. The chanting takes our external energy and transforms it into our inner consciousness. Meditation practice takes us to a different and higher level of awareness as we have discussed in our earlier meditation sessions.

Eternal Calmness Mantra:

The eternal AUM..... of quieting vibration and energy
AhhOomm...AhhOom...AhhOomm...AhhOomm....
AhhOomm....

Hatha Yoga Health Mantra:

Deep breath in....holding....exhaling.... Hamm...
Saaaa....Hamm...Saaaa
The idea is to get rid of the Carbon Dioxides in the body. It is pronounced:
Ham..Sa...Ham..Sa...Ham..Sa....Ham..Sa...Ham..
Sa...Ham..Sa
It is often used with Mudra or body movements as well. Meaning "I AM" in other words concentrating on self expression, I AM an active part of the

universal Law of eternal life, I AM connected to All that is, was or shall BE.

Christian Jesuit Mantra:

The Priests spend hours, days, weeks chanting just one word, the name of Jesus: Jes-u, Jes-u, Jes-u, Jes-u, Jes-u, Jes-u, Jes-u, Jes-u, Jes-u, Jes-u, Jes-u, Jes-u, Jes-u, Jes-u, Jes-u,

Hebrew or Jewish Orthodox Mantra:

Adoni, Go-Ho-Ho..My-Ho..Imm.. Go-Ho-Ho.. My-Ho..Imm....
Adnoni, Go-Ho-Ho..My-Ho..Imm.
Meaning: God the Holy, Holy Mighty, Holy and Immortal... God the Holy, Holy and Immortal... Externally hearing the Words, Internally thinking about the implication of the Words

Buddhist Chants:

Om Ma Ni Pad Me Hum...
A simple translation is "seeking the jewel in the Lotus."

Originally the Sanskrit mantra of Bodhisattva Avalokiteshvara of India, it later became the main Tibetan mantra of Chenrezig representing the Bodhisattva of Boundless Compassion. Tibetans believe this Bodhisattva is endowed with complete illumination, and refrains from entering the nirvana without residue, a state of eternal nirvana; instead vowing to be reborn here on Mother Earth, so he can continue to help save humanity. In this manner his written works continue to be guidance to the Mahayana Teacher/Messengers of the Buddha-way.

Om Ma Ni Pad Me Hum   Om Ma Ni Pad Me Hum
Om Ma Ni Pad Me Hum from the Heart Sutra

Here we have both the "Omm" and the "Hum" again. The pronunciation changes dependent on whether one is chanting in Chinese or Tibetan, as Tibetans do not pronounce d and hu's in the same manner as the Indians or Chinese. The pronunciation goes: Indian: Om MaNi Pad Me Hum or Tibetan: Om Mani Peme Hung

Another Tibetian Chant is:

Om Ah Hum.... Om Ah Hum.... Om Ah Hum....

It is believed that chanting this all will be transformed into natural purity. It brings together the empowerment of beginning, middle and end. Like other mantras it is in repetition that empowerment comes.

"Chanting is not so much about pronunciation, how fast or slow one chants, rather it is an offering of "consciousness communication" of humility, gratitude and sincerity, that raises our senses to a higher level of BE-ing, a connection to where we came from." HL

CHANTING as Meditation

This is a powerful mantra for Health, mind settling and empowerment. It is the main mantra for over thirty million people around the world chanting for spiritual sustain-ability and peaceful means by Mahayana Buddhists in the Nichiren tradition.

INFINITE TITLE OF THE LOTUS SUTRA:

Chanted in three methods: SLOW AND CHOIR LIKE:
Namu - MyoHo - Renge - Kyo, Namu - MyoHo - Renge - Kyo
[slow and song like chant]

MEDIUM AND EMPHASIS DRIVEN:
Nam - Myoho - Renge - Kyo   Nam - Myoho - Renge - Kyo Nam - Myoho - Renge - Kyo [rhythmic chanting]

FAST AND RYTHMIC:
Nam - Myoho - Renge - Kyo   Nam - Myoho - Renge - Kyo Nam - Myoho - Renge - Kyo [rhythmic chanting]

Mantra of Nichiren Daishonin [1222 - 1282 c.e.] originally of Japan

A SIMPLE MEANING:

Namu meaning an offering, Nam meaning a devotion: so a devotional offering to eternal universal Law - of the Buddha's teachings within the Lotus Sutra, through the sound of our beautiful voices, originally the voice of the Buddha.

Namu	= devotion offering and I take refuge in the Buddha
Myoho	= eternal, infinite, universal Law
Renge	= the teachings of the Buddha as per the Lotus Sutra
Kyo	= the sound of our beautiful voices, originally the voice of the Buddha

Go now and give it a try, do not worry about pronunciation, or whether you are chanting correctly or not; just do it and feel the powerful energy. Here is a suggested method: 5 minutes chanting with drum beat, 20 minutes chanting in harmony with lead chanter, ending with 5 minutes of chanting with drum beat, then 3 - 5 minutes of silence to bring us back to the present.

Sound Meditation to Vitalize
Mind, Body, Soul
Our Yogic Meditative Breath ~ Leading
to Spirit

Contemplative Mind

Five Methods

Practice of Loving Kindness

Meditation of a Thousand Ways

Tien Tai's Ten Ways of Meditation

More Meditation Exercises

*Ability to keep the mind on One Point
without wavering is called concentration;
this is far from easy" HL*

FIVE METHODS OF MEDITATION

1] Beginners Meditation – focus on Breath, yogic breath exercises, quiet mantra chanting
2] Visualization Meditation, focus on One Point, dependent origination, Oneness
3] Awakening of personal realization, Heart-Mindfulness
4] Meditation on Letting Go, Temporary Mind, Eternal Mind
5] Void, nothingness, reaching bliss and beyond

The realization then is that we are part of an inter-dependent eternal spirit that has taken on a body. From these meditative forms and daily practice come the seeds of One's consciousness, our thoughts and ideas about life, birth and so called death; we realize our conditional and temporal BE-ing. Using these Five Methods we can focus on our present existence: who am I, why am I here, what is important to me, do I realize how my meditations are the pathway to my true nature, meditating on inner self, that leads to awakening of One's eternal nature.

The Art and the Act of Meditation is a mindful practice that has the realization that everything comes from one's mind. HL

Making progress we are ready for the next stage of deep meditation as we focus our mindfulness on attachments and letting go of attachments, unconditional love, loving and letting go, neither here, nor there, understanding truly that life just is, the knowing of here and now, what is, what is not, existence, non-existence, cause, karma, and effect. This is the Buddha-way to realizing the pathway to liberation or freedom. Nirvana at the first level.

Consider Earth as the world of *samsara*, the land of endurance, realizing mind-energy is the river running through on the crossing to the heavens free of emotional BE-ing, nirvana, the release of sufferings.

Metta: sending forth meditative energy thoughts of goodwill and kindness to everyone you have met, past, present and future. *Karuna:* sending forth meditative energy of compassion and empathy to relieve the suffering of self and others *Mudita*: realizing blissful joy, we share our inner happiness, accept the joy of others without envy *Upekkha:* meditating on equality, environment of well being with non judgement

As we spend the hours and days of developing our meditative practice, we become ever more peaceful, with our busy mind, frustrations, angers, transformed into unconditional loving BE-ing. We are not surprised when others begin to come forward and ask where does your happiness come from, why is your demeanor so bright and light?

The next level is transformation of our human energy being free from emotion, the realization and vision of where I came from, where I AM, where I will go when I leave mother Earth, the light and energy of the universal Law; acceptance without worry or fear of death.

MEDITATION OF THE THOUSAND WAYS

What we have learned is that Meditation is a balance of awareness, concentration and energy. When we start meditating it becomes clear that everything is changing moment to moment, as the mind races from place to place like a ping pong ball in action. Our thought patterns change, the body shifts and demands attention; we find it hard to be still, energized and concentrated. Therefore, our meditations will be appropriate to the mood or condition we are in at the moment of practice. Our disposition will be determined by our posture, our approach, our attitude, our view, and by non-desire. The main factor is practice daily regardless of the kind of day one has had. Chanting through frustration or anger, chanting through sadness or sorrow, chanting with joy and happiness, chanting for health or wealth; but always chanting. This is the *Meditation of the Thousand Ways*. This Meditation brings the Five *Desired Powers*, empathy, understanding, compassion, mindfulness beyond temporary mind; at one with eternal mind

FIVE MOMENTARY MEDITATIONS

With this meditative practice, we move from beginning meditations to middle meditations which lead us to wondrous deeper meditation.

Allow us to begin considerations of insightfulness by removing obstacles to wisdom and enlightenment; non attachment, reality of the temporary nature of all things, contemplation on the meaning of eternal. Meditation on Light and Energy of the universal Law of life with all its meanings, beyond what we call death. We recognize this as the stages of progress; calming, controlling and cultivating our mind, realizing one's inter- dependent nature. All is One, we are free, we are becoming whole and holistic in our human form.

TIEN TAI'S TEN ACTS OF MEDITATION

1] Preparation of holy space, place of regular practice, including Five offerings: greens, incense, candles, water and food. If we are doing an outdoor walking exercise this can be set up at our starting and ending point.

2] Cleansing and stretching of body, dressing lightly, washing, bathing. During a Retreat this should be done up to three times a day as part of body meditation... "I am cleaning, purifying my body.. that my eternal spirit may see, smell, hear my efforts"

3] Chanting of an Opening Invocation and Closing Invocation

4] Calling on Bodhisattvas to come and join with us, offering protection and insight

5] InSightful Meditation we can circumnavigate to the Buddhas of the Ten Directions, which allows them to hear, see, our efforts to mature self and to assist others

6] Meditating on the six senses of everyday life, we offer thanksgiving for our human abilies.

7] Walking Meditation

8] Chanting or Sound Meditation

9] Awareness Meditation, calm, silent, deep meditative Joy

10] Peaceful activity.... discipline, holding the moment, working in our spiritual Diary aspiring to results

---

MEDITATION

As we have worked our way through our Sharing Sessions, we have found useful meditation exercises that have expanded our mindfulness and helped us along the pathway to silence. Here then are ten more practices that will assist us with personal growth, open mindedness and assist in going ever deeper towards the silence and the void, the colors and the visions of our meditations, moments from the Eighth

World of Realization, moments of wisdom, moments of enlightenment!

MEDITATION

These Exercises are simple ways of opening the
Pathways to deeper Meditation

M = MATURITY   E = ENERGY

D = DISCIPLINE   I = INFINITE

T = TALENT   A = ATTITUDE

T = TIMELESS   I = IMAGINATION

O = OBSERVATION   N = NIRVANA

MEDITATION

The Act of Meditation

20 Minutes A Day Out of 24 Hours
So Simple, So Difficult
Contemplation of Body, Mind & Spirit

The Art of Meditation

We Breath deeply, we Stretch the body, We Ask,
Seek, Learn, Realize

MEDITATION PATH: Respect
MEDITATION COMPASS: Maturity

M   MATURITY

– how mature am I

– where does my maturity come from

– how do I achieve deeper maturity

– how does maturity balance with my mindflness

We enter the silence, concentrating on these
insightful words. We listen, we see, we hear, we
observe, we respect, we let go, we meditate on
Maturity.

MEDITATION

The Act of Meditation

20 Minutes A Day Out of 24 Hours
So Simple, So Difficult
Contemplation of Body, Mind & Spirit

The Art of Meditation

We Breath deeply, we Stretch the body, We Ask,
Seek, Learn, Realize

MEDITATION PATH: Vital Life Force
MEDITATION COMPASS: Energy

E   ENERGY

– what is vital life force

– do I understand the fusion of self and eternal
energy

– energy source is health source

– how do I use energy to strengthen my faith

We enter the silence, concentrating on these
insightful words. We listen, we see, we hear, we
observe, we respect, we let go, we meditate on
Energy.

MEDITATION

The Act of Meditation

20 Minutes A Day Out of 24 Hours
So Simple, So Difficult
Contemplation of Body, Mind & Spirit

The Art of Meditation

We Breath deeply, we Stretch the body, We Ask, Seek, Learn, Realize

MEDITATION PATH: Knowledge
MEDITATION COMPASS: Discipline

D = DISCIPLINE

- lack of discipline leads to imbalance

– do I struggle with discipline

– how is my Health affected by discipline

– how do I realize the results that come from self discipline

We enter the silence, concentrating on these insightful words we listen, we see, we hear, we observe, we respect, we let go, we meditate on Discipline

MEDITATION

The Act of Meditation

20 Minutes A Day Out of 24 Hours
So Simple, So Difficult
Contemplation of Body, Mind & Spirit

The Art of Meditation

We Breath deeply, we Stretch the body, We Ask,
Seek, Learn, Realize

MEDITATION PATH: Time
MEDITATION COMPASS: Infinite

I = INFINITE

- what does infinite mean to me

- am I aware of the infinite energy within myself

- when I am mindful can I feel beyond the finite

- in the infinite can I find my sacred space

We enter the silence, concentrating on these
insightful words. We listen, we see, we hear, we
observe, we respect, we let go, we meditate on the
meaning of Infinite.

MEDITATION

The Act of Meditation

20 Minutes A Day Out of 24 Hours
So Simple, So Difficult
Contemplation of Body, Mind & Spirit

The Art of Meditation

We Breath deeply, we Stretch the body, We Ask,
Seek, Learn, Realize

MEDITATION PATH: Ability
MEDITATION COMPASS: Talent

T = Talent

- I meditate on my positive abilities

- I give thanks for my talents

- I quietly assess where I am in the here and now

- I listen to my inner voice

We enter the silence, concentrating on these
insightful words. We listen, we see, we hear, we
observe, we respect, we let go, we meditate on my
Talents.

MEDITATION

The Act of Meditation

20 Minutes A Day Out of 24 Hours
So Simple, So Difficult
Contemplation of Body, Mind & Spirit

The Art of Meditation

We Breath deeply, we Stretch the body, We Ask,
Seek, Learn, Realize

MEDITATION PATH: Life Force
MEDITATION COMPASS: Attitude

A = Attitude

- do I realize the life force my attitude holds

- is my attitude respectful toward Self

- how is my attitude toward others

- am I mindful daily of my attitude

We enter the silence, concentrating on these
insightful words. We listen, we see, we hear, we
observe, we respect, we let go, we meditate on my
Attitude.

MEDITATION

The Act of Meditation

20 Minutes A Day Out of 24 Hours
So Simple, So Difficult
Contemplation of Body, Mind & Spirit

The Art of Meditation

We Breath deeply, we Stretch the body, We Ask,
Seek, Learn, Realize

MEDITATION PATH: Knowing
MEDITATION COMPASS: Timeless

T = TIMELESS

- I meditate on how quickly time passes

- eternity means timeless universal energy

- quietly, I realize my own timelessness

- I offer loving, timeless compassion to family

We enter the silence, concentrating on these
insightful words. We listen, we see, we hear, we
observe, we respect, we let go, we meditate on the
meaning of Timeless eternity.

MEDITATION

The Act of Meditation

20 Minutes A Day Out of 24 Hours
So Simple, So Difficult
Contemplation of Body, Mind & Spirit

The Art of Meditation

We Breath deeply, we Stretch the body,
We Ask, Seek, Learn, Realize

MEDITATION PATH: Sacred Space
MEDITATION COMPASS: Imagination

I = INSPIRATION

- where does my inspiration come from

- I meditate on my visions

- I believe in my imagination

- where does my inspiration take me

We enter the silence, concentrating on these insightful words. We listen, we see, we hear, we observe, we respect, we let go, we meditate on my Inspiration.

MEDITATION

The Act of Meditation

20 Minutes A Day Out of 24 Hours
So Simple, So Difficult
Contemplation of Body, Mind & Spirit

The Art of Meditation

We Breath deeply, we Stretch the body,
We Ask, Seek, Learn, Realize

MEDITATION PATH: Awareness
MEDITATION COMPASS: Observation

O = OBSERVATION

- I meditate on how I observe all that is around me

- how non judgmental am I in my observations

- do I realize the importance of quiet time in observing

- BE-ing aware I can observe with more clarity

We enter the silence, concentrating on these insightful words. We listen, we see, we hear, we observe, we respect, we let go, we meditate on Observation.

MEDITATION

The Act of Meditation

20 Minutes A Day Out of 24 Hours
So Simple, So Difficult
Contemplation of Body, Mind & Spirit

The Art of Meditation

We Breath deeply, we Stretch the body, We Ask,
Seek, Learn, Realize

MEDITATION PATH: The Goal
MEDITATION COMPASS: NIRVANA

- nirvana comes in many levels

- we are aware that getting to nirvana means
letting go

- nirvana means end of suffering

- I meditate with gratitude in reaching
momentary nirvana

We enter the silence, concentrating on these
insightful words. We listen, we see, we hear, we
observe, we respect, we let go, we enter Nirvana,
if even just for a moment.

Quiet In Our Meditations

Meditation on Happiness and Peace

One's Spiritual Diary

Practice A Beautiful Habit

*"When the Student Is Ready the Teacher/
Messenger Will Appear"*

QUIET IN OUR MEDITATIONS

"I AM cultivating my miracle mind" HL

I am doing this by observing correct speech, talking little in my everyday activities, allowing no negative talk to enter my conversations. We all remember "if you can't say something nice, don't say anythingat all" Bambis mother. Buddha talk is exactly like this. It can calm my mind. I am doing this by listening carefully to what is in my mind, what do I see, what do I hear? I am taming my busy mind by meditating on Love, the pathway to enlightenment.

Good words build clarity of mind, this is essential for long term contemplative meditation. Faith, practice, and study build knowledge and wisdom in our meditations. With time we are relieved of the hindrances of a busy mind.

At the beginning, as we have seen over these weeks of study and practice, meditation is not an easy task which is why so few pursue it beyond looking into it, not realizing the great benefits that truly lead to freedom. Meditation transforms all into natural purity, filling one with generosity, skillful means and the desire to help relieve the suffering of others, the Bodhisattva way.

Over these sessions we calm the mind in the beginning, through our Breath Exercise, which leads to Mantra Exercise, which leads to Visualization of

One Point, One Object of a meditation, which leads to letting go and finding eternal bliss.

MEDITATION ON HAPPINESS AND PEACE

Meditation is a fresh look at life, as we seek more tranquillity and insight so we will better relate to all life's challenges and its gifts of love and happiness. Meditation enables us to see clearly what is important and what we should let go. The Wheel of change is the only thing permanent, acceptance of change is our challenge.

Having a healthy mind of skepticism, questioning purpose and motivation of that which presents itself is right, good and natural. Through meditative insight we find our intuition true, our fears false, our worries gone, gone like the wind passing through.

Time is on our side. Life-time is eternal. Time existing in the moment of Now. We embrace our inner feelings, check our motivation that our actions be beneficial. Meditate with hope for a better self and better world that peaceful means may come.

Come to understand delusion is an illusion awaiting Right Knowledge. Right Speech and Right Views come with Right Meditation. Wisdom and enlightenment come with Right Action.

Meditation brings security and empowerment, having shifted in our knowing, we become firm in our resolve to answer all of life's challenges in the best possible way. Our discipline strengthens the mind, our practice strengthens resolve. The rewards are ours. Climbing the mountain of meditation, One is enriched with a deeper view of the territory we call life. With a fresh view, the reward of a seeking mind, we awaken our inner voice without self seeking, wisdom arising, enlightenment on the horizon.

Through taming our busy mind, we seek Mindful ways. Through good words, clarity in our hearing, seeing, with faith, wisdom and rightful knowledge, we accept freedom from hindrances. These efforts hard to come by, with attention to the detail and respect in the realization of the words of our teacher, mentor.

In Mindfulness we observe correct speech, talking little, we cut off negative talk, we listen to what is in our temporary mind; what do I see, what do I hear, we are cultivating the mind in meditating on Love.

With realization and practice of One's meditation techniques, one will now quickly attain and enter Mindfulness, and herein find the world of purity, discovery of inner self, happiness, kindness, love, compassion and, in this realm we remain protected when all around is in chaos.

If we question "what am I meditating on"? The answer comes soon enough. We are meditating on our own mind, cultivating and learning to control it. We are observing our thought impulses, calming them, resting them, letting them go, so that we may be at peace.

Our Spiritual Diary

How many years I have used the 3 X 5 cards in my pocket, by my bedside, how beautiful is my cover bound Spiritual Diary, that place where I write down the expanded version of my meditative thoughts. This is such an important part of the balance of action, memory, and growth as we daily work towards our dreams, visions, and working out the Five Challenges of this life, Family, Relationships, Career, Health of Body, Mind and Spirit, and Economics or Money. As we have seen in our daily meditation practice, we are often offered the Voice of our conscious communication with the universal Law and our connection with the Eternal Memory.

We are human, so a good discipline is to listen carefully and take a few notes then expand on them later. This way we do not lose important messages. Listening to our intuition is vital to avoiding suffering and pain. Of course, Now I simply put a few words into my smart phone, and expand them into my Spiritual Diary later.

Practice A Beautiful Habit

We end by coming back to the beginning. We find that *Meditation*, the *Art and Act of Mindfulness* is a practice of discipline, endurance and simplicity. For Visualization, we can gaze at a candle and the blue light therein, we can observe a mandala, we can offer our breath count, we can watch our breath; as beginning points of letting go, leading us to boundless meditations.

We realize once again that the only constant is change, we become empowered to control the mind, instead of the emotional, busy mind controlling us. We come to realize in the deeper level of our meditations we hardly know we are breathing, we are at peace in the Oneness of the moment, without time or space hindering us.

Lower Level: meditating on friendship, compassion, joy. Middle Level: meditating on equality, blissfulness, mindfulness, love. Higher Level: meditating on temporary nature, universal nature, oneness with the universal Law and our Eternal Memory, located at the Eighth Level of Consciousness.

We realize all energy comes and goes, filled with electro-magnetic fields we can communicate with and through. Science has come to realize, we become filled with a personal empowerment to let go and just be, enjoying the bliss of practice, coming back to earth to pick up the day. Our Buddha-nature is in tune with all that is in the here and now. Past, present and future become One. May your meditations be strong, healthy and rewarding!

Namaste, the Spirit in Me, See's the Spirit in You, and it is Good
N.Henry Landry, Author, Buddhist Teacher/ Messenger

Nichiren Peace Center offers several Retreats Annually

Visit www.VIRetreats.com for Annual Schedule

Everyone Welcome, we have two Retreat Huts for rental

And several Tent spaces at our Two Hectors/Acre Vancouver Island Retreat Garden

If you have enjoyed this book you may be Interested in Buddha Nature Now by the same Author, this is a lay persons guide to the Buddhist Philosophy.

ISBN: 978 - 1 - 4259 - 9914 - 8 [prt]
ISBN: 978 -1 -4678 -0939 - 9 [E]

Printed in the United States
By Bookmasters